STATIONS OF THE CROSS FOR CHILDREN

JULIANNE M. WILL
ILLUSTRATED BY PATRICIA MATTOZZI

Our Sunday Visitor Publishing Division
Our Sunday Visitor, Inc.
Huntington, Indiana 46750

Dedication

For my mom and dad, Darrell and Sue Will,
who first started me on the journey.

=>·•·<=

Nihil Obstat: Rev. Michael Heintz
Censor Librorum

Imprimatur: ✠ John M. D'Arcy
Bishop of Fort Wayne-South Bend
April 27, 2005

The *Nihil Obstat* and *Imprimatur* are official declarations that a book or pamphlet
is free from doctrinal or moral error. It is not implied that those who have
granted the *Nihil Obstat* and *Imprimatur* agree with the contents, opinions, or
statements expressed.

The Scripture citations used in this work are taken from the *Catholic Edition of the
Revised Standard Version of the Bible* (RSV), copyright © 1965 and 1966 by the
Division of Christian Education of the National Council of the Churches of Christ
in the United States of America. Used by permission. All rights reserved.

Every reasonable effort has been made to determine copyright holders of
excerpted materials and to secure permissions as needed. If any copyrighted
materials have been inadvertently used in this work without proper credit being
given in one form or another, please notify Our Sunday Visitor in writing so that
printings of this work may be corrected accordingly.

Our Sunday Visitor Publishing Division
Our Sunday Visitor, Inc.
200 Noll Plaza
Huntington, IN 46750

ISBN: 1-59276-153-4 (Inventory No. X204)

Cover and interior design by Rebecca Heaston
Cover and interior art by Patricia Mattozzi

PRINTED IN THE UNITED STATES OF AMERICA

INTRODUCTION TO THE STATIONS OF THE CROSS

I'm so happy you will be joining me on this journey.

That's what the Stations of the Cross are — a journey. For Jesus, the journey was real. He had to walk down a long, dusty road carrying a heavy cross. At the end of that road, soldiers nailed Jesus to the cross. They thought he was lying about being the Son of God. Jesus died on that cross.

For us, the Stations of the Cross are a prayer journey. We read these fourteen stations to learn about what happened to Jesus when he died. When we see how much Jesus suffered, we realize just how much he loved us. We can say prayers of thanks and love every step of his way. When things are tough in our own lives, we can imagine what it was like to be in Jesus' sandals. We can remember that after all Jesus went through, God raised him from the dead and took him to heaven.

During Lent, we walk on this journey with Jesus. As we pray, we imagine what it was like to be there when Jesus takes the rough, heavy cross. We see Jesus when he falls, three times, because he is hurt and tired. We go with Jesus to the top of the hill, where they nail him to the cross. We walk this sad journey with Jesus because he did it for us, to help make up for our sins.

This journey goes to a wonderful place: heaven. On Easter, we remember that God raised Jesus from the dead, and we celebrate. Because Jesus died on the cross, he opened the door to heaven for us. When we walk with him, Jesus will lead us through that door to joy forever.

— JULIANNE WILL

First Station
Jesus Is Condemned to Death

We adore you, O Christ, and we praise you, because by your holy cross you have redeemed the world.

Dear Jesus,

You must have felt so scared when they told you that you were going to die on the cross.

Sometimes I feel scared about things I have to do. I feel nervous and worried, and I wish it would all just go away. Help me be brave just as you were, Jesus. Help me tell the truth, and help me do what I know I need to do. I know you always love me and protect me. Please remind me just how close you are when I am scared.

Amen.

SECOND STATION
JESUS TAKES UP HIS CROSS

We adore you, O Christ, and we praise you, because by your holy cross you have redeemed the world.

Dear Jesus,

The cross they gave you to carry was so rough and heavy. It hurt your hands and shoulders right from the start. And it was so big, you had to drag it step-by-step. The road ahead was very long, and at the end you were going to die. Your journey must have seemed impossible. Even so, you reached out and took the cross.

Share your strength with me, Jesus, when I have to do a big project or a hard chore. I will remember how you took the cross without complaining or running away. Help me be as strong as you when I have to face my responsibilities. Teach me to do my work with your grace.

Amen.

Third Station
Jesus Falls the First Time

We adore you, O Christ, and we praise you, because by your holy cross you have redeemed the world.

Dear Jesus,

It really hurt when you fell down with the heavy cross. It probably hurt your feelings, too, when some of the people teased you because you fell. It must have been so hard to get up.

When I fall, it hurts in lots of ways. Sometimes I get a bruise, and sometimes I also feel really embarrassed. I'm glad you're with me, Jesus, when I fall, to help me get back up and dust myself off. You make me feel better in every way, because I know you love me and you care about me.

Amen.

FOURTH STATION
JESUS SEES HIS MOTHER, MARY

We adore you, O Christ, and we praise you, because by your holy cross you have redeemed the world.

Dear Jesus,

Your mother was always there for you. She stood by the road while you carried the cross, even though it broke her heart to see you hurting. It must have made you feel so much better to see her then. Mary knew you needed her love.

Thank you for the people who love me, Jesus. They make me feel safe and happy when things go wrong. I will do my best to show them how much I love them, too. Please bless them with your grace and protection.

Amen.

FIFTH STATION
SIMON OF CYRENE HELPS JESUS CARRY HIS CROSS

We adore you, O Christ, and we praise you, because by your holy cross you have redeemed the world.

Dear Jesus,

I wonder what Simon must have thought when the soldiers grabbed him from the crowd and made him help you. He didn't know you, and he saw everyone teasing and hurting you. I wonder whether he felt scared. I wonder whether he felt bad for you. I wonder whether he felt glad he could help you.

Simon's hands and shoulders made things easier for you for a little while. Thank you, Jesus, for the people in my life who make things easier for me when I am having a hard time. Thank you for the times when you have been by my side. Please give me strong shoulders and a strong heart, so I can make things easier for people who need help.

Amen.

Sixth Station
Veronica Wipes Jesus' Face

We adore you, O Christ, and we praise you, because by your holy cross you have redeemed the world.

Dear Jesus,

Veronica was very brave. She knew that most of the people in the crowd hated you because you called yourself the Son of God. She knew they wanted to punish your friends, too. But Veronica saw that you were sweaty and dirty and bleeding, so she wiped your face with her cloth.

Jesus, teach me how to be brave like Veronica. Show me how to help someone who is in trouble, even if all my friends are teasing that person. Show me how to care for someone who is hurt. Even if I can't fix the problem, I can be nice and make someone feel better. Thank you, Jesus, for making me feel better when I need to feel loved.

Amen.

SEVENTH STATION
JESUS FALLS THE SECOND TIME

We adore you, O Christ, and we praise you, because by your holy cross you have redeemed the world.

Dear Jesus,

There are times when I really, really feel like giving up. It's tough to try again when something doesn't go right. Sometimes it seems as if the work is just too hard. Sometimes it feels as if I'm just not good enough. It would be easy to go do something else.

But you were able to get up and try again even after you fell twice. It was really hard for you, too. It would have been easier to say you were wrong and give up. But you knew how very important it was for God's plan. Some things are just that important. Thank you for showing me how to keep trying. I will remember you when I fall down or things go wrong — even if they go wrong twice.

Amen.

Eighth Station
Jesus Meets the Women of Jerusalem

We adore you, O Christ, and we praise you, because by your holy cross you have redeemed the world.

Dear Jesus,

The women of Jerusalem were so sad for you. They cried and cried because you had to carry the cross. They were scared because you were going to die. But you told them, "Do not weep for me." You trusted that God the Father would make everything okay in the end.

Sometimes I feel very scared because I don't understand what's happening in my life. Bad things sometimes happen, and I don't know how it will get better. But I know there are people who will take care of me. Even more important, I know that you will watch over me. I know I can always pray to you when I feel like crying.

Amen.

Ninth Station
Jesus Falls the Third Time

We adore you, O Christ, and we praise you, because by your holy cross you have redeemed the world.

Dear Jesus,

It was a good thing you were almost at the end of the road when you fell the third time. You must have been so tired and in so much pain. Some of your friends were very sad, because they knew that when you got to the end you were going to die on the cross.

But you trusted that after you died on the cross, God the Father would make everything okay. Even though it seemed like a really sad time to your friends, you knew that you would be able to be with them in a deeper way than before. Some things are like that: They seem terrible until we understand why. People who have faith believe that God has a reason for everything. Jesus, help my faith grow, so that even when things seem terrible, I will trust that God can make everything okay.

Amen.

Tenth Station
Jesus Is Stripped of His Clothes

We adore you, O Christ, and we praise you, because by your holy cross you have redeemed the world.

Dear Jesus,

The soldiers were trying to do everything they could to hurt and embarrass you. They even took your clothes and rolled dice to see who could have them. They were not treating you like the Son of God.

I'm sorry for the times I have made someone else feel embarrassed. When I hurt them, I hurt you, too. Please forgive me for the times I was mean. I will remember to treat everyone just as I would treat you. And please forgive those people who have made me feel embarrassed. Help them remember to treat me and others as they would treat you, too.

Amen.

ELEVENTH STATION
JESUS IS NAILED TO THE CROSS

We adore you, O Christ, and we praise you, because by your holy cross you have redeemed the world.

Dear Jesus,

I can't imagine how much pain you suffered when they nailed your hands and feet to the cross. Even worse, people around you were teasing you. They said you should save yourself if you were really the Son of God. One prisoner, who was on a cross beside you, believed in your power. Because he believed, he got a place in heaven. Your mother, Mary, and your disciple John were there with you, too, even as you were hanging from the cross. It must have been so hard for them to watch you suffer.

I will try to be like Mary and John when my friends or family need me. I will be there when it's really hard to see them hurt so much. And I want to be like that prisoner who believed. I know that you are with me now, Jesus, and I want to be with you, too.

Amen.

TWELFTH STATION
JESUS DIES ON THE CROSS

We adore you, O Christ, and we praise you, because by your holy cross you have redeemed the world.

Dear Jesus,

When the ground started to shake, the sun stopped shining, and the curtain in the Temple tore in two, some people became very scared. When you died on the cross, some of them realized what a terrible mistake they had made. They realized you weren't a liar, and they went home very afraid.

I have made mistakes, too. I know that I need to try to fix my mistakes and do better the next time. I have to tell people I am sorry. I also have to tell you I am sorry. Thank you, Jesus, for all the times you have forgiven me for my mistakes. Thank you for the love you show me. I love you, too, Jesus.

Amen.

Thirteenth Station
Jesus Is Removed from the Cross

**We adore you, O Christ, and we praise you,
because by your holy cross you have
redeemed the world.**

Dear Jesus,

A man named Joseph of Arimathea was kind and brave to take your body down from the cross. He knew that some people still thought you were a liar and hated you and your friends. But Joseph wanted to show his love for you. So he carefully wrapped you in a soft cloth, just as he would do for someone in his own family.

It is easy to give someone my extra things or to help them when I have extra time. It is very hard to help someone when I don't have extra things or extra time. Please show me how to give, even when it is hard. I know this would make you very happy, just as Joseph must have made God the Father very happy.

Amen.

FOURTEENTH STATION
JESUS IS BURIED

We adore you, O Christ, and we praise you, because by your holy cross you have redeemed the world.

Dear Jesus,

Your friends must have been very sad when Joseph of Arimathea rolled that giant stone in front of your tomb. As they sat outside the cave, they probably wondered what to do next. They didn't have a leader anymore. There were many people who hated them for being friends with you. They would have missed you very much.

Sometimes I feel very lonely. Sometimes my friends or parents are mad at me. Sometimes I don't know anyone in a new place. I'm so glad that you are always by my side, Jesus. I know that you are always my friend. I will never be alone. I want to follow you, Jesus, as I make my own journey through life.

Amen.

EASTER
THE REST OF THE STORY

Jesus' friends went back to his tomb on the third day to watch and pray. But when they arrived, they were surprised to see that the giant stone had been moved. They looked inside, but Jesus was nowhere to be found.

Instead, the friends saw two angels. The angels told them that Jesus was not there because he had risen from the dead. Jesus' friend Mary Magdalene was frightened, but then she saw Jesus, and he told her that he was alive. She ran to tell the rest of Jesus' friends.

They didn't know what to think. They didn't believe Mary. But Jesus visited again one day, walking with two of his friends to a town called Emmaus. Later, he joined all his friends in a room where they were hiding, trying to decide what to do next. That's when his friends knew: Jesus had really risen from the dead! His power — God's power — was stronger than death.

Jesus sent his friends out to tell the world this wonderful news. They went on many journeys to spread the Good News. Jesus wants us to make that same journey today!